KID_food_

RACHAEL RAY

30-MINUTE MEALS

♦

Published by:
Lake Isle Press, Inc.
16 West 32nd Street, Suite 10-B
New York, NY 10001
(212) 273-0796
E-mail: lakeisle@earthlink.net

Distributed to the trade by:
National Book Network (NBN), Inc.
4501 Forbes Boulevard, Suite 200
Lanham, MD 20706
1 (800) 462-6420
www.nbnbooks.com

Library of Congress Control Number: 2005929075

ISBN: 1-891105-22-1

Food photography copyright © 2005 Tina Rupp

Book and cover design: Ellen Swandiak

This book is available at special sales discounts for bulk purchases as premiums or special editions, including personalized covers. For more information, contact the publisher at (212) 273-0796 or by e-mail, lakeisle@earthlink.net

First Edition

Printed in China

For picky eaters everywhere

RACHAEL RAY

TOP 30

30-MINUTE MEALS

Just getting meals on the table every night is a challenge, but you do it, anyway you can. It's an even greater challenge to keep meals simple and appealing, day after day. Am I right? Let these meals help you break the routine. Super Sloppy Joes, Eggplant Roll-Ups, and Broccoli and Bow Ties, for example, may just get you out of that cooking rut. With their broad appeal, kids will love 'em. I've written them just for you!

RACHAEL RAY

30-MINUTE MEALS

**DON'T MEASURE WITH
INSTRUMENTS, USE YOUR
HANDS.**

You're not baking or conducting
experiments for the government—
just feel your way through.

HOW TO MEASURE RACHAEL'S WAY:

A HANDFUL
about 3 tablespoons

A PALMFUL
about 2 tablespoons

HALF A PALMFUL
you do the math

A PINCH
about 1/4 teaspoon

A FEW GOOD PINCHES
about 1 teaspoon

ONCE AROUND THE PAN
about 1 tablespoon of liquid

TWICE AROUND THE PAN
more math: about 2 tablespoons,
3 or 4 would be 1/4 cup

RACHAEL RAY

TOP 30

30-MINUTE MEALS

DILLY OF A QUESADILLA

SERVE *with* GREEN SALAD

makes 4 servings

DILLY of a QUESADILLA

Salsa:

6 firm plum tomatoes, diced

1/4 medium white onion, chopped fine

A palmful cilantro leaves, finely chopped

1 serrano pepper, seeded and minced (see Note)

Coarse salt, to taste

2 pieces boneless, skinless chicken breasts

1/2 pound chorizo (Spanish smoked sausage), or
   substitute andouille, linguica, or spicy kielbasa

1 tablespoon smoky barbecue sauce

8 large flour tortillas

12 ounces shredded Mexican cheese blend (see Note)

Combine all salsa ingredients.

Heat griddle or nonstick skillet to high. Cook chicken and
chorizo for 4 minutes on each side. Remove from heat.
Dice chorizo and chicken.

In a small bowl, coat the chicken with barbecue sauce.

Wipe off griddle and return to medium-high heat. Blister
each tortilla for 30 seconds on the first side, then flip.
Place a little chicken, chorizo and cheese on 1/2 of the
tortilla's surface. Fold the other half over the top of the fill-

ing. Press down with a spatula. Flip the quesadilla over and cook for another 30 seconds. Remove.

Cut each quesadilla into 4 wedges and top with a sprinkle of salsa. Repeat. Each quesadilla should be on the grill for only 2 minutes or so. Serve with green salad on the side. Makes 8 quesadillas.

Note: Serranos look like tiny jalapenos and are widely available in produce sections.

Note: Asadero, Monterey Jack, and cheddars. Available in the dairy aisle of your market.

RACHAEL RAY

TOP 30

30-MINUTE MEALS

PIZZA *with* CHICKEN, SUN-DRIED TOMATOES & BROCCOLI *aka* "THE ONLY PIZZA YOU'LL EVER WANT"

CHEESY POPCORN

makes 4 servings

KIDfood

PIZZA with Chicken, Sun-Dried Tomatoes & Broccoli

Crust:

1 package (16 ounces) pizza dough, at room temperature

2 teaspoons extra-virgin olive oil

2 tablespoons grated Parmigiano Reggiano or Parmesan cheese

Toppings:

1/3 pound trimmed broccoli, about 1/3 head

1 tablespoon extra-virgin olive oil

3 cloves garlic, cracked

1/3 pound chicken breast (cut for stir fry) or chicken tenders

Salt and freshly ground black pepper, to taste

1 cup part-skim ricotta cheese

10 sun-dried tomatoes in oil, drained and sliced

1 cup shredded mozzarella cheese

12 to 15 leaves fresh basil, torn or stacked and thinly sliced

Preheat oven to 500°F.

On a 12-inch nonstick pizza pan, stretch out the dough and form the crust. Drizzle 2 teaspoons olive oil onto crust and spread with a pastry brush to the edges. Sprinkle with Parmigiano Reggiano or Parmesan cheese.

In a small covered saucepan, bring 2 inches water to a boil. Separate broccoli tops into florets; discard lower stalks or reserve for a soup. Salt water and add broccoli florets. Cook covered, 3 to 5 minutes. Drain, set on cutting board, and chop florets into small pieces.

Heat a small nonstick skillet over medium-high heat. Add oil, garlic, and chicken. Season with salt and pepper. Brown chicken until lightly golden, 5 minutes, then transfer chicken and garlic to a cutting board and chop into small pieces.

To assemble pizza, dot crust with chopped broccoli, garlic and chicken. Add spoonfuls of ricotta throughout and spread gently with the back of a spoon. Add sliced sundried tomatoes, scattering them around the pizza to the edges. Top with a thin layer of shredded mozzarella. Place pizza in oven on middle rack and lower heat to 450°F. Bake 10 to 12 minutes, until cheese is deeply golden and crust is brown and crisp at the edges. Remove from oven and let stand 5 minutes. Top with lots of basil. Cut pizza into 8 slices and serve.

CHEESY POPCORN

2 tablespoons vegetable oil
1 cup popping corn kernels
3 tablespoons melted butter
1/2 cup grated Parmesan cheese

Heat oil in deep pot over medium-high heat. Add corn.
Cover pot and pop the corn, shaking pan often. Remove
from heat. Drizzle with melted butter and sprinkle evenly
with cheese. Serve hot. Makes 4 BIG servings.

RACHAEL RAY

TOP 30

30-MINUTE MEALS

GRILLED 4-CHEESE SANDWICHES

MEATBALL & MACARONI SOUP

makes 4 BIG servings

KID food

Meatball & Macaroni **SOUP**

2 tablespoons extra-virgin olive oil

2 carrots, peeled and chopped

2 ribs celery, chopped

1 medium onion, chopped

2 bay leaves, fresh or dried

Salt and freshly ground black pepper, to taste

1 pound ground beef, pork, and veal combined

1 egg beaten

2 cloves garlic, minced

1/2 cup grated Parmigiano Reggiano or Romano cheese

1/2 cup plain bread crumbs

1/2 teaspoon freshly grated or ground nutmeg

6 cups chicken stock or broth

2 cups water

1 & 1/2 cups dried pasta: rings, broken fettuccini or ditalini

1 pound triple-washed fresh spinach, coarsely chopped

In a deep pot over medium heat, add oil, chopped carrots, celery, onions, and bay leaves. Season with salt and pepper. Cover pot and cook 5 or 6 minutes, stirring occasionally.

While veggies cook, combine ground meats, egg, garlic, grated cheese, bread crumbs, salt, pepper, and nutmeg.

Add broth and water to the pot of veggies. Increase heat to high and bring soup to a boil, then reduce heat a bit and start to roll meat mixture into small balls, dropping them straight into the pot. When done rolling the meat, add pasta to the soup and stir. Cover and simmer soup, 10 minutes. Remove bay leaves. When pasta is tender, stir in chopped spinach in batches. When spinach has wilted, the soup is done and ready to serve. Adjust seasonings, and serve with crusty bread or grilled 4-cheese sandwiches.

"Yumm-o!"

GRILLED 4-CHEESE Sandwiches

2 tablespoons extra-virgin olive oil

3 tablespoons butter

1 clove garlic, cracked away from the skin

8 slices crusty Italian semolina bread

1 cup shredded provolone cheese

1 cup shredded mozzarella cheese

1/2 cup grated Parmigiano Reggiano or Romano cheese

1 cup shredded Asiago cheese

In a small skillet over medium-low heat, combine oil, butter, and garlic, and cook gently for 2 or 3 minutes, then remove from heat.

Place a large nonstick skillet on the stove over medium-high heat. Using a pastry brush, brush one side of 4 slices of bread with garlic and butter oil and place buttered side down in skillet. Top each slice with equal amounts of the 4 cheeses. Top each sandwich with another slice of bread, and brush with garlic butter. Flip the sandwiches a few times until cheeses are melted and gooey and bread is toasty and golden. Cut sandwiches from corner to corner and serve.

RACHAEL RAY

TOP
30

30-MINUTE MEALS

TUSCAN-STYLE CHICKEN CUTLETS

CREAMY SPINACH

makes 4 servings

KIDfood

Tuscan-Style CHICKEN CUTLETS

1 & 1/3 to 1 & 1/2 pounds chicken breast cutlets
2 large plastic food storage bags
3 large eggs, beaten
1 cup all-purpose flour
1 teaspoon poultry seasoning
Coarse salt and black pepper, to taste
Vegetable or extra-virgin olive oil, for frying
1 large lemon, cut into wedges

Place cutlets in large food storage bags a few inches apart and lightly pound to 1/4-inch thickness.

Beat eggs in a shallow dish. Mix flour, poultry seasoning, salt, and pepper in a second dish.

Place a cookie sheet in oven on low heat, about 275ºF.

Heat 1/2 inch oil in a large, deep skillet over medium heat.

Coat chicken in flour, shaking off excess. Remove pieces one at a time. Coat each cutlet in egg, draining off excess. Add cutlets to oil, 2 or 3 at a time, and brown 'til lightly golden, 3 minutes on each side. Place cutlets in oven on low and repeat process until all the cutlets are done. Serve with lemon wedges and creamy spinach.

"I always say K.I.S.S.—Keep It Super Simple.**"**

Creamy **SPINACH**

1 & 1/2 bags (16 ounces) triple-washed spinach
1 tablespoon extra-virgin olive oil
1/2 tablepoon butter
1 medium shallot, peeled and chopped fine
1 1/2 tablespoons all-purpose flour
1 cup reduced-fat milk
3 ounces reduced-fat cream cheese, softened
2 or 3 pinches nutmeg (1/4 teaspoon)
Coarse salt and black pepper, to taste

Sort spinach leaves and remove large, tough stems.
Coarsely chop and set aside.

Heat a deep skillet over medium to medium-low heat.
Add oil and butter. When butter melts, add shallot and
sauté 2 or 3 minutes. Whisk in flour and cook a minute
more. Add milk and whisk until smooth. Add cream
cheese and whisk until melted. Add nutmeg. Add
spinach to the pan in stages. Turn spinach in sauce, and
as it wilts, add more and more greens. Season with salt
and pepper.

RACHAEL RAY

TOP
30

30-MINUTE MEALS

HOMEMADE
CHICKEN & STARS SOUP

SERVE *with* CRUSTY BREAD

makes 4 servings

Homemade
CHICKEN & STARS SOUP

2 quarts (8 cups) chicken broth

1 pound boneless, skinless chicken breast or chicken tenders

1 bay leaf, fresh or dried

2 medium carrots, peeled and chopped or thinly sliced

2 ribs celery (from heart of stalk), chopped

1 medium onion, finely chopped

1 cup star-shaped egg pastina pasta

Freshly ground black pepper, to taste

Suggested garnishes:

Grated Parmigiano or Romano cheese

Chopped fresh flat-leaf parsley

Oyster crackers

Crushed saltines

Croutons

Plain popcorn or white cheddar popcorn

In a large pot, heat 1 quart (4 cups) broth to boiling. Add chicken and bay leaf, and simmer, covered, about 8 minutes. Add vegetables as you chop them. Remove chicken after 8 minutes and place on a cutting board to cool.

Add the second quart of broth to your pot and bring to a boil. Add pasta and cook 6 minutes. Remove pot from heat. Dice chicken, add to pot, and season with pepper to taste. Remove bay leaf. If soup is too thick, add up to 2 cups of water for desired consistency. Top with your choice of garnishes and serve with crusty bread.

RACHAEL RAY

TOP 30

30-MINUTE MEALS

PEASANT PASTA

SERVE *with* CRUSTY BREAD

makes 4 to 6 servings

Peasant PASTA

1 pound bulk Italian sweet sausage
1 can (28 ounces) chunky-style crushed tomatoes
1/2 cup frozen green peas
1/2 cup heavy cream or half-and-half
1/2 pound penne rigate, cooked until al dente
Grated Parmigiano Reggiano cheese, for the table

In a large skillet over medium heat, brown sausage and drain fat. Wipe out skillet and return to heat. Add cooked sausage crumbles back to pan and add tomatoes. Bring to a bubble and cook for 5 minutes. Add peas and cook for 1 minute more. Stir in cream, to blush the color of the sauce. Simmer until pasta is ready to drain. Toss two-thirds of the sauce with pasta and transfer to serving bowl. Top with remaining sauce and serve with grated cheese and crusty bread.

RACHAEL RAY

30-MINUTE MEALS

SCUDERI KIDS' FAST FAKE-BAKED ZITI

SERVE with **CRUSTY BREAD** and **GREEN SALAD**

makes 6 servings

KID food

Scuderi Kids' Fast
FAKE-BAKED ZITI

3 tablespoons extra-virgin olive oil

3 cloves garlic, finely chopped

1 can (28 ounces) whole peeled tomatoes, preferably San Marzano

1 can (14 ounces) crushed tomatoes, preferably San Marzano

Salt and freshly ground black pepper, to taste

A handful of fresh basil leaves, torn

1 pound ziti rigate

2 tablespoons butter

2 tablespoons all-purpose flour

A generous grating of fresh nutmeg

2 cups whole milk

1/2 cup shredded Asiago cheese

1/2 cup shredded Parmigiano Reggiano cheese

1 cup cubed fresh mozzarella cheese

Put a large pot of water on to boil. Preheat the broiler.

Heat a medium saucepan over medium heat; add evoo, then garlic. Sauté a minute or two; do not let the garlic brown. Chop whole tomatoes and add them to the pan. Add crushed tomatoes and salt and simmer 10 minutes. Add basil and simmer over low heat 10 minutes more.

When water boils, add salt and pasta and cook 6 minutes, leaving pasta a little chewy.

While pasta cooks, make the béchamel sauce: Melt butter in a small pot over medium heat. Whisk in flour, then salt, pepper, and nutmeg; cook 1 minute. Stir in milk and bring sauce to a bubble. Cook 5 minutes to reduce.

When pasta is cooked, drain and transfer to a big casserole dish. Pour the tomato and basil sauce over the pasta and turn to coat. Pour the béchamel over pasta—do not mix. Top with Asiago, Parmigiano, and mozzarella. Place the casserole under hot broiler and melt cheese until brown and bubbly, 3 to 5 minutes. Serve immediately, with crusty bread and green salad on the side.

Note: If San Marzano tomatoes are not available, you might want to add a teaspoon of sugar to your sauce.

RACHAEL RAY

TOP 30

30·MINUTE·MEALS

SHRIMP SCAMPI *on* ANGEL HAIR PASTA

makes 4 to 6 servings

KIDfood

SHRIMP SCAMPI
on Angel Hair Pasta

1 pound angel hair pasta, cooked al dente to package
directions

2 pounds large, raw shrimp, peeled and deveined under
running water, butterflying as you devein by cutting
lengthwise into shrimp, almost splitting them

1 cup all-purpose flour

2 teaspoons ground thyme or Old Bay seasoning

Coarse salt and freshly ground black pepper, to taste

1/2 cup extra-virgin olive oil

6 cloves garlic, popped from skin and minced

1 cup dry white wine

1 large lemon

1 cup canned chicken broth

A couple drops Worcestershire sauce

3 tablespoons butter

A handful fresh flat-leaf parsley, finely chopped

"You're never too young to be in the kitchen."

Pat shrimp dry with paper towels. Mix flour with a little ground thyme or Old Bay seasoning, salt, and pepper in a shallow dish. Lightly coat shrimp in seasoned flour.

Pour olive oil into a deep, heavy-bottomed skillet over high heat. Cook shrimp in a single layer, in 2 batches if necessary. Sauté each batch 2 or 3 minutes, until edges are golden. Remove shrimp and place on paper towel–lined plate. Pour off any excess oil.

Return pan to heat. Add garlic, then wine to the pan and scrape up any bits from the bottom. Reduce wine by half. Roll lemon on counter with a back-and-forth motion to release its juices. Split lemon in half. Add broth, Worcestershire, and the juice from the lemon halves. Let the sauce simmer and reduce for 2 or 3 minutes. Stir in butter with a whisk or fork.

Season with more salt and pepper. Add the shrimp back to sauce and remove from heat. Give the pan a shake. Sprinkle with parsley and serve with crusty bread for dunking or pour over a bed of angel hair pasta cooked al dente—with a bite.

RACHAEL RAY

30-MINUTE MEALS

SPICY CHICKEN TACOS

makes 6 servings

Spicy Chicken **TACOS**

1 & 1/2 pounds boneless, skinless chicken breasts, cut into small cubes

1 tablespoon extra-virgin olive oil

1 small onion, chopped

1 clove garlic, minced

1 cup tomato puree

2 teaspoons chili powder

1 teaspoon ground cumin

A handful coarsely chopped Spanish olives stuffed with pimientos

A handful golden raisins

Coarse salt, to taste

8 jumbo corn taco shells, or 8 flour tortillas for soft tacos

Toppings:

Shredded cheeses:
  smoked cheddar, Monterey Jack, or pepper-Jack

Avocado dices

Tomato dices

Chopped green onion

Shredded lettuce

In a big skillet over medium heat, brown chicken in olive oil. Add onion and garlic and cook another few minutes to soften onion. Add tomato puree, chili powder, cumin, olives, raisins, and salt, to taste. Bring to a bubble, reduce heat to low, and simmer until ready to serve.

Warm taco shells or flour tortillas in oven according to package directions.

Scoop filling into shells and add toppings at the table.

RACHAEL RAY

TOP
30

30-MINUTE MEALS

CHICKEN & DUMPLINGS

SERVE *with* GREEN SALAD

makes 6 servings

CHICKEN & DUMPLINGS

2 boneless, skinless chicken breasts, 4 pieces, up to 2
  pounds

1/2 cup all-purpose flour

Coarse salt and white or black pepper, to taste

2 tablespoons extra-virgin olive oil

2 ribs celery, trimmed, halved lengthwise, then coarsely
  chopped

1 medium white onion, chopped

1 white potato, peeled and diced

2 carrots, peeled and diced

1 box Jiffy biscuit mix

A handful fresh flat-leaf parsley, chopped

3 cans (14 ounces each) low-sodium chicken broth

1 cup water

"Cooking rocks!"

Cut chicken into big chunks. Spill a handful or two of flour onto a shallow dish. Salt and pepper the flour. Toss and roll the chicken chunks in the flour to coat. Discard the extra flour and wash hands.

To give the dumplings room to cook, divide ingredients and cook in 2 separate pans. Heat a little oil in each of 2 skillets over medium-high heat. Place chicken pieces in hot pans and brown 4 minutes on each side. Remove from pans and reduce heat to medium. Add chopped veggies and sauté for 2 or 3 minutes, giving the pans a shake now and then.

While veggies cook, mix up 1 box of Jiffy biscuit mix, adding a handful of parsley to the batter. Add 1 & 1/2 cans chicken broth and 1/2 cup water to each pan. Add chicken back to pans. Bring liquids to a boil. Drop in biscuit mix a heaping tablespoon at a time, 5 or 6 dumplings per pan. Cover with foil or lids and simmer 8 to 10 minutes. Uncover and cook an additional 3 to 5 minutes or until sauce thickens to desired consistency. Adjust salt and pepper to taste. Serve with a green salad.

RACHAEL RAY

TOP
30

30-MINUTE MEALS

DEVILISH CHILI-CHEESE DOGS

SUMMER-ISH SUCCOTASH SALAD

makes 4 servings

KIDfood

Devilish CHILI-CHEESE DOGS

1 tablespoon extra-virgin olive oil

1 pound ground sirloin

Salt and freshly ground black pepper

2 teaspoons Worcestershire sauce

1 small onion, chopped

2 cloves garlic, chopped

1 tablespoon chili powder

1 can (8 ounces) tomato sauce

8 fat or foot-long beef franks

1 tablespoon butter

1 tablespoon hot sauce, such as Tabasco

8 hot dog buns, toasted

2 cups (10-ounce sack) shredded cheddar cheese

Heat a medium skillet over medium-high heat. Add evoo and meat and season with salt and pepper. Brown and crumble beef. Add Worcestershire, onion, garlic, and chili powder; cook together 5 minutes. Add tomato sauce and reduce heat to low.

Boil franks in a shallow skillet of water to warm through, 5 minutes. Drain and return pan to medium heat. Score casings on dogs. Melt butter in skillet and add hot sauce.

Add dogs to skillet, browning and crisping the casings in hot sauce and butter.

Preheat broiler. Place dogs in buns and top with chili and lots of cheese. Place under broiler and melt cheese. Serve immediately.

Summer-ish SUCCOTASH Salad

2 cups frozen corn kernels, thawed
1 can (15 ounces) butter beans, drained
1 small red bell pepper, chopped
1/2 small red onion, chopped
1 tablespoon red wine vinegar
2 tablespoons chopped fresh flat-leaf parsley
2 tablespoons peanut or vegetable oil
Salt and freshly ground black pepper, to taste

Combine corn, beans, bell pepper, and onion and toss with vinegar, parsley, oil, salt, and pepper. Serve with chili-cheese dogs.

◆ ◆ ◆ ◆ ◆ **12** ◆ ◆ ◆ ◆ ◆

RACHAEL RAY

TOP 30

30-MINUTE MEALS

NEW ENGLAND TASTY TUNA MELT

SERVE *with* CHIPS *and* GREEN SALAD

makes 4 servings

New England Tasty TUNA MELT

4 sandwich-size sourdough English muffins
2 large cans (9 ounces each) tuna in water, well-drained
5 rounded tablespoons sweet pickle relish
1/2 medium white onion, finely chopped
2 ribs celery with leaves, finely chopped
2 teaspoons Old Bay seasoning
1/2 cup mayonnaise or ranch dressing
4 radishes, finely chopped
Salt and freshly ground black pepper, to taste
2 vine-ripened tomatoes, sliced
3/4 to 1 pound sharp white cheddar cheese, sliced

Preheat broiler. Place English muffins on a cookie sheet; lightly toast, then remove from oven. Leave the broiler on.

Mix tuna with relish, onion, celery, Old Bay, mayo, and radishes, using 2 forks to combine and mash the salad. Season with salt and pepper. Use a large scoop to mound salad evenly on top of the 8 muffin halves. Top each mound with tomato and cheese slices and place the open-faced sandwiches under the broiler to melt the cheese. Serve immediately with chips of choice or green salad on the side.

RACHAEL RAY

TOP
30

30-MINUTE MEALS

BROCCOLI & BOW TIES

SERVE *with* GREEN SALAD *and* CRUSTY BREAD

makes 4 to 6 servings

KIDfood

"My family taught me about life through food.**"**

BROCCOLI & BOW TIES

1 cup water

1 pound broccoli florets or broccolini florets, coarsely chopped

1/4 cup extra-virgin olive oil

5 cloves garlic, minced

3 pinches crushed red pepper flakes

1 pound bow-tie pasta, cooked until al dente

1/2 cup grated Parmigiano Reggiano cheese

A handful chopped fresh flat-leaf parsley

1/4 teaspoon ground nutmeg

Coarse salt and black pepper, to taste

Bring a cup of water to a boil in a medium pan and reduce heat to simmer. Add florets, cover pan, and steam 3 to 5 minutes, 'til tender. Drain and set aside.

Heat olive oil in a deep, nonstick skillet over medium heat. Add garlic and crushed red pepper flakes. When garlic speaks by sizzling in oil, add florets and sauté 1 or 2 minutes. In the pan or in a large bowl, toss the florets with pasta, cheese, parsley, nutmeg, salt, and pepper. Transfer to a serving dish and serve with a green salad and crusty bread.

RACHAEL RAY

TOP 30

30-MINUTE MEALS

MAPLE MUSTARD PORK CHOPS
with GRILLED APPLES

MOM'S OIL & VINEGAR
POTATO SALAD

makes 4 servings

KID*food*

Mom's Oil & Vinegar
POTATO SALAD

16 new red potatoes
Coarse salt
1 red bell pepper, seeded and chopped
1/2 medium red onion, chopped
1/4 cup chopped fresh mint
1/4 cup chopped fresh flat-leaf parsley
3 tablespoons red wine vinegar
1/3 cup extra-virgin olive oil
Salt and freshly ground black pepper, to taste

Put potatoes in a pot, cover with water, replace lid, and bring to a boil over medium-high heat. Add a liberal amount of coarse salt and cook until potatoes are just tender, about 12 minutes. Remove from heat, drain, and cold shock them until just cool enough to handle. Coarsely chop and return them to the warm pot. Add bell pepper, onion, mint, parsley, and vinegar to the pot and toss until potatoes absorb the vinegar. Add oil and stir until the potatoes mash up a bit and salad has a spoon-able consistency. Season with salt and pepper and transfer to a serving bowl. Makes 4 BIG servings.

Maple Mustard PORK CHOPS
with Grilled Apples

1/2 cup dark amber maple syrup

4 tablespoons spicy brown mustard (1/4 cup)

1/4 cup apple cider

1/4 medium onion, finely chopped

1/2 teaspoon allspice

1 teaspoon ground cumin

8 center-cut boneless pork loin chops, 1/2 to 3/4-inch thick

Extra-virgin olive oil, for drizzling

Montreal Grill Seasoning by McCormick or salt and pepper, to taste

3 Golden Delicious apples, sliced across into 1/2-inch rounds, with core and peel intact

The juice of 1/2 lemon

1/2 teaspoon freshly grated or ground nutmeg

Preheat grill or nonstick griddle pan over medium-high heat, or preheat electric table top grill to high. Also, preheat oven to 350°F.

Combine maple syrup, mustard, cider, onion, allspice, and cumin in a small saucepan and cook over moderate heat, 7 to 10 minutes, until sauce begins to thicken a bit.

Coat chops lightly in oil, season with grill seasoning blend or salt and pepper, and cook on the grill, 3 minutes on each side. Baste chops liberally with sauce and cook, 2 or 3 minutes more, then transfer to a baking sheet. Baste again with sauce and place in a hot oven to finish cooking them. Bake 10 to 12 minutes, until your apples are ready to come off the grill pan.

Coat apple rounds with lemon juice and a drizzle of oil. Season with grill seasoning or salt and pepper, and a little nutmeg. Cover grill with as many pieces of apple as possible. As they get tender, remove and replace with remaining slices. Apples should cook 3 minutes on each side, as you don't want them too soft, just tender. Serve chops alongside apples.

✦ ✦ ✦ ✦ ✦ **15** ✦ ✦ ✦ ✦ ✦

RACHAEL RAY

TOP 30

30-MINUTE MEALS

HOT BUFFALO CHICKEN SANDWICHES

SUPER STUFFED POTATOES *with* THE WORKS

makes 4 servings

SUPER STUFFED POTATOES
with **The Works**

4 slices center-cut bacon, chopped

2 all-purpose potatoes, such as russet

1/2 cup regular or reduced-fat sour cream

2 scallions, finely chopped

Salt and freshly ground black pepper, to taste

1 cup shredded cheddar, Colby, or smoked cheddar
   cheese

In a small nonstick skillet over medium-high heat, brown bacon pieces, then drain on paper towel.

Pierce potatoes a few times each with a fork. Microwave on high for 12 minutes. Let potatoes cool a few minutes before handling.

Preheat broiler.

Carefully split potatoes and scoop out flesh into a small bowl. Combine with sour cream, scallions, salt, pepper, and cheese. Scoop back into the potato skins and place under broiler to lightly brown the tops and serve, allowing 1/2 potato per person.

Hot Buffalo CHICKEN Sandwiches

4 pieces boneless, skinless chicken breast
  (about 6 ounces each)

Salt and freshly ground black pepper, to taste

1 teaspoon sweet paprika

1 teaspoon chili powder

A drizzle extra-virgin olive oil

2 tablespoons butter

1/2 cup (4 ounces) hot sauce, such as Frank's Red Hot

4 crusty rolls, split

Bibb or leaf lettuce leaves

2 cups reduced-fat sour cream

4 scallions, thinly sliced

1/2 pound blue cheese, crumbled

8 ribs celery, cut into sticks

2 large carrots, peeled, and cut into sticks

"These are fun foods—have fun with them!"

Heat a large nonstick skillet over medium-high heat. Season chicken with salt, pepper, paprika, and chili powder. Drizzle with a little olive oil to coat. Pan grill, 5 minutes on each side.

Heat a medium metal or oven-safe glass bowl over low heat to melt the butter. Add hot sauce to the butter and combine. When the chicken breasts are done, remove from pan and add to the bowl and coat evenly with the hot sauce mixture.

Place chicken breasts on bun bottoms and top with crisp lettuce.

Combine sour cream, scallions, and blue cheese and slather on bun tops. Top sandwiches and serve, using remaining sauce for dipping veggies. Arrange on dinner plates with stuffed potatoes, celery, and carrot sticks.

RACHAEL RAY

30-MINUTE MEALS

SESAME NOODLES

SERVE *with* FRUIT *or* CHUNKED SALAD

makes 4 servings

◆ ◆ ◆ ◆ ◆ **16** ◆ ◆ ◆ ◆ ◆

Sesame NOODLES

1/4 cup low-sodium soy sauce

2 tablespoons tahini (see Note)

2 tablespoons toasted sesame oil (in Asian foods aisle)

2 pinches cayenne pepper

2 cloves garlic, minced

1 inch gingerroot, grated, or 2 pinches ground ginger

1 pound cappellini (angel hair pasta) cooked al dente

3 scallions, sliced thin on an angle

1 large carrot, peeled and grated

Toasted sesame seeds and crushed red pepper flakes,
   for garnish

Combine soy sauce, tahini, sesame oil, cayenne, garlic,
and gingerroot in a bowl. Whisk until smooth.

Drain cooked pasta and run under cold water to chill.
Drain very well, giving several good, strong shakes.

In a large bowl, toss noodles with dressing until evenly
coated with a thin layer of sauce. Add veggies and transfer to a serving dish. Garnish with sesame seeds and a
little crushed red pepper flakes. Serve with fruit or a
chunked vegetable salad.

Note: A paste made from ground sesame seeds—tahini
can be found in the international or natural food aisles.

RACHAEL RAY

TOP 30

30-MINUTE MEALS

MEATZA PIZZA BURGERS

SERVE *with* CHUNKED VEGETABLE SALAD

makes 4 servings

"Appeal to your own taste buds."

Meatza Pizza BURGERS

3/4 pound very lean ground beef
2 tablespoons tomato paste
1/4 pound chopped chorizo or pepperoni
Chopped fresh oregano, to your taste
2 cloves garlic, minced
Black pepper, to taste
4 slices provolone cheese
Romaine lettuce
1 firm tomato, sliced
4 round, crusty, sesame rolls

Combine ground beef, tomato paste, chorizo or pepperoni, oregano, garlic, and pepper. Form into 4 patties. Cook burgers for 5 minutes on each side over medium-high gas heat or charcoal. In the last minute, melt a slice of provolone on each burger. Place in rolls and top with romaine and sliced tomato. Serve with a chunked vegetable salad.

RACHAEL RAY

TOP 30

30-MINUTE MEALS

ZESTY CHICKEN CUTLETS PARMIGIANA

SERVE *with* GREEN SALAD

makes 4 servings

KIDfood

Zesty CHICKEN CUTLETS Parmigiana

1 pound spaghetti

Quick marinara sauce:

3 cloves garlic, minced

2 pinches crushed red pepper flakes

2 tablespoons extra-virgin olive oil

2 cans (28 ounces each) crushed tomatoes

15 to 20 leaves fresh basil, roughly cut or torn

2 sprigs fresh oregano, leaves stripped from stem and chopped

A handful chopped fresh flat-leaf parsley

Cutlets:

The juice of 3 lemons

1/3 cup freshly grated Parmigiano Reggiano or Romano cheese

1 cup Italian bread crumbs

Freshly ground black pepper, to taste

A pinch crushed red pepper flakes

A handful chopped fresh flat-leaf parsley

2 pounds boneless, skinless chicken breast cutlets

2 cloves garlic, popped from skin and left whole

3 tablespoons extra-virgin olive oil

1 pound fresh mozzarella or fresh smoked mozzarella, thinly sliced

"Mamma mia, this is a party!"

Bring a large pot of salted water to boil for pasta. When ready, cook pasta until al dente, or still slightly firm to the bite.

Throw sauce together by heating garlic and crushed red pepper in olive oil over medium heat. When garlic speaks by sizzling in oil, add tomatoes and basil, oregano, and parsley. Bring to a bubble, reduce heat, and let the sauce hang out over low heat while you prepare cutlets.

Squeeze lemon juice into a shallow dish. Mix Parmigiano, bread crumbs, black pepper, red pepper, and parsley on a large plate. Turn each cutlet in lemon juice, then press and coat in breading.

Heat 2 whole cloves garlic in olive oil in a large skillet or frying pan over medium heat. When garlic sizzles, remove garlic and sauté chicken cutlets 4 minutes on each side. When cutlets are done, arrange on an ovenproof serving dish covered with a layer of sauce. Dot each cutlet with a little more sauce and a slice of fresh mozzarella. Place platter under broiler just until cheese melts.

Take warm platter right to the table. Toss drained spaghetti with remaining sauce and serve as a side dish along with green salad. Enjoy!

RACHAEL RAY

TOP 30

30-MINUTE MEALS

PESTO PIT-ZAS
with SPINACH & BROCCOLI

SERVE *with* GREEN SALAD

makes 4 servings

"30 minutes and a little imagination can take you to Italy, Spain, Hong Kong, and beyond.**"**

PESTO PIT-ZAS

with **Spinach & Broccoli**

4 (8-inch) pita breads

1/2 cup basil pesto, homemade or storebought (available on dairy aisle)

1 cup part-skim ricotta cheese

1 cup cooked broccoli florets, chopped

1 package (10 ounces) frozen chopped spinach, defrosted and squeezed dry

2 cloves garlic, finely chopped

Salt and pepper, to taste

2 cups shredded mozzarella

Preheat oven to 400°F.

Toast pita bread on cookie sheets, 2 to 3 minutes. Remove from oven and set aside.

Combine pesto, ricotta, broccoli, spinach, and garlic. Season with salt and pepper. Top each pita with 1/4 of the mixture, then top with mozzarella. Return pizzas to the oven and bake, 12 minutes, or until cheese bubbles and begins to brown. Serve with green salad on the side.

RACHAEL RAY

30-MINUTE MEALS

FETTUCCINE ALL'ALFREDO

SERVE with GREEN SALAD

makes 4 servings

KIDfood

FETTUCCINE *all'* ALFREDO

1 package (12 ounces) egg fettuccine
3 tablespoons butter
1 cup heavy cream or half-and-half
1 cup grated Parmigiano Reggiano cheese
1/4 teaspoon freshly grated or ground nutmeg
Coarse salt and freshly ground black pepper, to taste

Bring salted water to a rolling boil for your pasta and cook to package directions. Drain well.

Preheat a large skillet over medium heat, add butter and melt. Add cream or half-and-half, and stirring constantly, add cheese and cook, 1 minute. Season with nutmeg, a pinch of salt, and pepper. Turn off heat and add drained pasta to the skillet, tossing until pasta is evenly coated. Adjust seasonings and serve with green salad on the side.

RACHAEL RAY

TOP 30

30-MINUTE MEALS

ITALIAN PATTY MELTS

CREAMY
TOMATO-BASIL SOUP

makes 4 servings

KID food

Creamy TOMATO-BASIL SOUP and ITALIAN PATTY MELTS

Soup:

4 cups whole milk

3 cans (14 ounces each) diced tomatoes, drained

2 rounded tablespoons tomato paste

1 medium onion, chopped

Salt and freshly ground black pepper, to taste

1 teaspoon sugar

1/4 cup all-purpose flour

2 tablespoons butter, cut into pieces

1 rib celery, coarsely chopped

1 clove garlic

1/2 cup store-bought basil pesto (available on dairy aisle)

Patty melts:

1 tablespoon extra-virgin olive oil, plus more for drizzling

4 sweet Italian sausage patties (1/4 pound each)
    (available in packaged meat case)

1 cubanelle (sweet Italian pepper), seeded and sliced

1 medium onion, sliced

Salt and freshly ground black pepper, to taste

8 slices sliced Italian bread

8 slices provolone cheese

Make the soup: Pour milk into a medium pot over medium heat and heat until hot but not boiling. Put tomatoes, tomato paste, onions, salt, pepper, sugar, flour, butter, celery, and garlic in a food processor and grind until smooth. Pour mixture into hot milk and raise heat to bring to a boil. Reduce heat and simmer 15 minutes.

Start the patty melts: Heat a nonstick skillet over medium-high heat. Drizzle pan with evoo and add sausage patties; cook 5 minutes on each side. Remove from pan and add another tablespoon evoo and the peppers and onions. Season with salt and pepper and cook until just tender, about 5 minutes. Remove from pan. Wipe pan clean and reduce heat to medium-low.

Assemble the sandwiches: Place 4 slices bread on a work surface, top each with 1/4 of the peppers and onions, then a slice of cheese, a sausage patty, another slice of cheese, and another slice of bread. Add butter to skillet and cook patty melts until golden and cheese is melted, 2 or 3 minutes on each side. Press with spatula as they cook or set another heavy skillet on top to weigh them down.

Pour soup into shallow bowls and stir a couple of rounded spoonfuls of pesto into each serving. Cut the patty melts corner to corner and dip in the soup as you eat.

◆ ◆ ◆ ◆ ◆ **22** ◆ ◆ ◆ ◆ ◆

RACHAEL RAY

TOP 30

30-MINUTE MEALS

WEEKNIGHT
SPAGHETTI & MEATBALLS

SERVE *with* GARLIC BREAD

makes 4 servings

Weeknight
SPAGHETTI & MEATBALLS

1 pound ground beef, 93% lean

1 egg, beaten

1/2 small cooking or boiling onion, finely chopped

2 cloves garlic, minced

1/4 cup grated Parmigiano Reggiano, plus more for the table

1/2 cup Italian bread crumbs

Freshly ground black pepper, to taste

1 tablespoon extra-virgin olive oil

1/2 cup beef broth or dry red wine

1 can (28 ounces) crushed tomatoes

1/2 teaspoon crushed red pepper flakes

2 sprigs fresh oregano, chopped, or 2 pinches dried

A palmful chopped fresh flat-leaf parsley

3/4 pound spaghetti, cooked until al dente

"Food can be a scrapbook of your life and times.**"**

Combine meat, egg, onion, garlic, grated cheese, bread crumbs, and a little pepper in a bowl.

Heat a deep nonstick skillet over medium-high heat and drizzle in oil. Roll small balls and drop into hot pan. When all the meatballs are in the pan, give the pan a good shake and cover. Cook for 8 minutes, giving the pan a good shake frequently to keep meat from burning. If balls are browning too quickly, reduce heat a little.

Add broth or wine and let reduce for 1 or 2 minutes. Add tomatoes and red pepper flakes, then oregano and parsley. Simmer until pasta is ready. Toss pasta with sauce and serve with garlic bread and grated cheese for topping.

RACHAEL RAY

30-MINUTE MEALS

ALASKA BURGERS

SERVE *with* CHIPS *and* GREEN SALAD

makes 4 servings

Alaska **BURGERS**

1 pound 93% lean ground beef

1/2 medium Spanish onion, minced or processed

4 shakes Worcestershire sauce

1/4 teaspoon allspice

1/2 teaspoon ground cumin

Cracked black pepper

1/3 pound (minimum) brick of smoked cheddar cheese,
  cut into 1/2-inch slices

1 tomato, cut into thick-slices

Lettuce for topping

4 fresh, crusty onion rolls

Mix beef, onion, Worcestershire, allspice, cumin, and black pepper in a bowl. Separate a quarter of the beef mixture. Take a slice of smoked cheese and form the patty around the cheese. Patties should be no more than 3/4-inch thick. Repeat, for a total of 4 patties.

Heat a nonstick griddle or frying pan to medium hot. Cook burgers 5 to 6 minutes on each side. Meat should be cooked through and cheese melted. (An instant-read thermometer should register an internal temperature of 170°F for well done or check the color by cutting into the meat.)

Add salt to taste. (Salting beef before cooking draws out juices and flavor.) Place in split rolls and top with tomato slices and lettuce. Serve with chips of choice and green salad on the side.

RACHAEL RAY

30-MINUTE MEALS

CASHEW! GOD BLESS YOU CHICKEN *with* JASMINE RICE

makes 4 servings

Cashew! God Bless You CHICKEN

with Jasmine Rice

1 box jasmine rice

1 pound boneless, skinless chicken breast, diced

2 tablespoons sesame oil

2 cloves garlic, minced and mashed

2 tablespoons rice wine, rice vinegar, or dry sherry

A couple of shakes crushed red pepper flakes

Freshly ground black pepper, to taste

1 large carrot, peeled and diced into small cubes

1 red bell pepper, seeded and diced

1 can (about 7 ounces) sliced water chestnuts, drained and coarsely chopped

3 heaping tablespoon-size scoops hoisin sauce (see Note)

A couple handfuls unsalted cashews (from the bulk candy and nuts section of the market)

3 green onions, thinly sliced on an angle

"Make weekday meals seem like special occasions.**"**

Following directions on box, start rice.

In a large bowl, combine chicken with 1 tablespoon sesame oil, garlic, rice wine, crushed red pepper, and black pepper. Set aside and let it hang out.

Heat remaining 1 tablespoon sesame oil in wok or large nonstick skillet over high heat until it smokes. Add carrot and stir-fry for 2 or 3 minutes. Add the coated chicken and cook another 3 or 4 minutes. Toss in the bell pepper and water chestnuts. Heat through for 1 minute. Add the hoisin and toss to coat evenly. Place chicken on a bed of jasmine rice and top with cashews and green onions. Feeds 4 well.

Note: An Asian condiment, similar to barbecue sauce, available in many markets in the Asian foods aisle.

RACHAEL RAY

TOP
30

30-MINUTE MEALS

MAC & CHEDDAR CHEESE
with **CHICKEN & BROCCOLI**

CHOPPED ICEBERG LETTUCE *with* "FRENCH" DRESSING

makes 6 servings

KIDfood

MAC & CHEDDAR CHEESE
with Chicken & Broccoli

2 tablespoons extra-virgin olive oil

1 pound chicken tenders, chopped

Salt and freshly ground black pepper, to taste

1 small onion, chopped

1 pound macaroni elbows or cavatappi

2 & 1/2 cups raw broccoli florets

3 tablespoons butter

3 tablespoons all-purpose flour

1/2 teaspoon cayenne pepper

1 teaspoon paprika

3 cups whole milk

1 cup chicken broth

2 & 1/2 cups (one 10-ounce sack) shredded sharp
   yellow cheddar cheese

1 tablespoon Dijon mustard

Place a large pot of water on to boil for pasta.

Meanwhile, heat a medium skillet over medium-high heat. Add evoo and chicken and season with salt and pepper. Sauté a couple of minutes then add onion; cook until onions are tender and chicken is cooked through, 5 to 7 minutes. Turn off heat and reserve.

To boiling water, add salt, then pasta. Cook 5 minutes, then add broccoli and cook for about 3 minutes.

While pasta cooks, make a roux: Heat a medium saucepan over medium heat. Add butter and let melt, then add flour, cayenne, and paprika and whisk together until roux bubbles, then cook a minute more. Whisk in milk and broth and raise heat a little to bring sauce to a quick boil. Simmer to thicken, 5 minutes.

Drain pasta and broccoli florets. Add back to pot along with chicken and onions.

Add cheese to milk sauce and stir to melt it in, a minute or so. Stir in mustard and season with salt and pepper. Pour sauce over chicken, broccoli, and cooked pasta, stirring to combine. Adjust seasonings, transfer to a large serving platter, and serve.

"Making a meal for yourself and your kids is real soul food."

CHOPPED ICEBERG LETTUCE
with "French" Dressing

1 head iceberg lettuce, cored and chopped
4 radishes, chopped
4 scallions, chopped
1/3 seedless cucumber, chopped
1 cup shredded carrots (preshredded available)

Dressing:
1/3 cup white wine vinegar
1/3 cup sugar
1/2 cup ketchup
1/2 cup extra-virgin olive oil
1 teaspoon garlic powder
2 teaspoons Worcestershire sauce
1/4 small white onion, finely chopped or grated
Salt and white pepper, to taste

Combine lettuce, radishes, scallions, cucumber, and carrots in a large salad bowl.

Make the dressing: Put all of the dressing ingredients in a blender. Blend on high with the top in place until combined. Pour dressing over salad and toss. Adjust salt and pepper.

RACHAEL RAY

30-MINUTE MEALS

WHITE LIGHTNING CHILI

makes 4 to 6 servings

White Lightning CHILI

1 tablespoon extra-virgin olive oil

2 pounds ground turkey breast

1 large yellow-skinned Spanish onion, chopped

1 serrano or jalapeño pepper, seeded and minced

2 cloves garlic, minced

2 tablespoons ground cumin

A couple shakes hot sauce, such as Tabasco

A palmful chopped fresh cilantro

2 cans (14 ounces each) low-sodium chicken broth

1 can (15 ounces) Great Northern/white kidney beans, drained

Coarse salt, to taste

Crushed tortilla chips for topping

Suggested garnishes:

Shredded Monterey Jack, pepper-Jack, or smoked cheddar cheese

Chopped green onions

Diced yellow tomatoes

"I look at the task at hand and say, 'I can figure this out.'"

Heat oil in deep skillet or pot over medium-high heat. Add turkey and cook for a couple of minutes, keeping the meat moving. Add onion, minced hot pepper, garlic, cumin, hot sauce, and cilantro. Reduce heat to medium and cook 5 minutes to soften and sweeten onion. Add broth and beans. Add salt to taste. Bring to a boil. Reduce heat and simmer until ready to serve.

Top bowls of chili with crushed tortillas—a great thing to do with those crumbs at the end of every bag. To really jazz it up, melt shredded Monterey Jack, pepper-Jack, or smoked cheddar over the top of each bowl and garnish with chopped green onions, and diced yellow tomatoes.

variation: **Who Ya Callin' Chicken?**
CHUNKY CHICKEN WHITE CHILI

Substitute 2 pounds of diced boneless, skinless chicken breasts for ground turkey breast and follow same method.

RACHAEL RAY

TOP 30

30-MINUTE MEALS

ELSA'S EGGPLANT ROLL-UPS

SERVE *with* GREEN SALAD

makes 4 servings

"Cooking is loose—
a little of this and a
little of that.**"**

Elsa's EGGPLANT ROLL-UPS

Vegetable or olive oil, for frying

2 medium Sicilian eggplants (smaller than regular, bigger than Japanese)

3/4 cup flour

Coarse salt and black pepper, to taste

3 eggs beaten, or 3/4 cup pasteurized egg substitute

Filling:

1 pound fresh mozzarella, or fresh smoked mozzarella, diced

20 leaves fresh basil

2 cups marinara sauce, homemade or jarred

Chopped fresh parsley, for garnish

Heat 1/2 inch oil in a large skillet over medium-high heat.

Thinly slice eggplants lengthwise. Place flour in a shallow dish, and season with salt and pepper. Dredge slices lightly in flour, then coat in egg. Fry 2 minutes on each side until golden, then transfer to paper towel-lined plate.

Drain excess oil from pan, wipe, and return to heat.

Top each eggplant slice with a basil leaf, diced cheese, and then roll up. Place bundles back in pan. Top with sauce. Reduce heat to low. Cover and cook 8 minutes. Top with parsley and serve with green salad on the side.

RACHAEL RAY

TOP
30

30-MINUTE MEALS

MEATLOAF PATTIES *with*
5-MINUTE SMOKY GRAVY

SMASHED POTATOES
with **SCALLIONS**

SERVE *with* **GREEN SALAD**

makes 4 servings

KID*food*

MEATLOAF PATTIES
and SMASHED POTATOES
with Scallions

Potatoes:

8 to 10 small white- or red-skinned potatoes, quartered

1/2 cup regular or reduced-fat sour cream

2 splashes low-fat milk (about 1/4 cup)

2 tablespoons butter

4 scallions, thinly sliced

Coarse salt and pepper, to taste

Patties:

1/2 cup plain bread crumbs

1 teaspoon ground cumin

1/2 teaspoon allspice

1 splash low-fat milk (about 1/8 cup)

1 large egg, beaten

1 small boiling onion, chopped fine

1 tablespoon Worcestershire sauce

1 rounded tablespoon tomato paste

A handful chopped fresh flat-leaf parsley

1 pound 90% lean ground beef sirloin

A drizzle extra-virgin olive oil or nonstick cooking spray

Gravy:

2 tablespoons butter

2 tablespoons all-purpose flour

1 can (14 ounces) low-sodium beef broth

2 tablespoons smoky barbecue sauce

1 rounded tablespoon tomato paste

Freshly ground black pepper, to taste

Bring a medium-size deep pot of salted water to a boil. Add potatoes and cook 10 to 12 minutes, 'til fork tender. Drain and return to hot pot. Add sour cream, milk, butter, and scallions and smash to desired consistency with potato masher. Season with salt and pepper.

While potatoes cook, combine the bread crumbs, cumin, and allspice in a large bowl. Add the milk, egg, onion, Worcestershire sauce, tomato paste, parsley, and beef. Mix together and form 4 large, oval-shaped patties, 1-inch thick.

Preheat a large nonstick skillet over medium-high heat. Add a little oil or nonstick cooking spray. Add patties to pan and cook 5 to 6 minutes. Flip patties, reduce heat, and cook 10 minutes more. Remove from pan.

To make gravy, add butter to pan and melt. Sprinkle in flour and cook over medium heat 1 to 2 minutes, whisking. Slowly add broth, stirring until combined. Bring to a boil. Reduce broth, 2 to 3 minutes. Whisk in barbecue sauce and tomato paste. Remove from heat and season with black pepper. Cover with aluminum foil until ready to serve.

Serve patties and potatoes with generous amounts of gravy and a green salad.

RACHAEL RAY

TOP 30

30-MINUTE MEALS

**PHILLY STEAK
SANDWICHES**

**SUPREME PIZZA
PASTA SALAD**

makes 4 servings

PHILLY STEAK Sandwiches

Onions:

1 tablespoon extra-virgin olive oil

2 large yellow onions, sliced very thin

Coarse salt and freshly ground black pepper or steak
    seasoning blend, to taste

Meat:

2 teaspoons extra-virgin olive oil, 2 drizzles

1 & 1/4 pounds lean beef tenderloin or sirloin, very
    thinly sliced, like carpaccio (ask butcher to do this)

1 teaspoon garlic salt

Coarsely ground fresh black pepper, to taste

8 slices provolone cheese

4 soft Italian hoagie rolls, each 6 to 8 inches long, split
    lengthwise

Heat a medium saucepan over medium-high heat. Add olive oil, onions, and salt and pepper or steak seasoning blend. Cook, stirring occasionally, 10 minutes or until onions are soft and caramel in color.

Heat a heavy griddle pan over medium-high to high heat. Wipe griddle with a drizzle of oil using a paper towel. Sear and cook meat until brown but not crisp, about 2 minutes on each side. Cook in single layers in two batches and tenderize by cutting into meat with the side of your spatula as they cook. When browned, just before you remove them from heat, sprinkle with garlic salt and pepper. When all are cooked, line each of your split rolls with 2 slices of cheese. Pile 1/4 of your meat and onions onto the griddle and mix together with your spatula. Remove and pile the meat and onions on top of the cheese, which will melt from the heat. Repeat for remaining servings and serve.

Supreme Pizza PASTA SALAD

1 pound wagon wheel pasta, cooked al dente, cooled
  under cold water, then drained

Salad:

2 plum tomatoes, seeded and chopped

1/2 medium red onion, chopped

8 fresh white button mushrooms, sliced

1 small green bell pepper, seeded and chopped

1 stick pepperoni, casing removed and cut into small dice

1 pound fresh mozzarella cheese or fresh smoked
  mozzarella cheese, diced

20 leaves fresh basil, torn or thinly sliced

Dressing:

1 teaspoon garlic salt

1 teaspoon dried oregano leaves or Italian dried seasoning

1 rounded tablespoon tomato paste

2 tablespoons red wine vinegar

1/3 cup extra-virgin olive oil

Freshly ground black pepper, to taste

Combine tomatoes, onion, mushrooms, bell pepper, pepperoni, mozzarella, basil, and pasta in a big bowl. In a medium bowl, whisk garlic salt, oregano or Italian seasoning, tomato paste, and vinegar together. Stream in olive oil while continuing to whisk. When oil is incorporated, pour dressing over pasta salad, add a few grinds of black pepper, then toss to coat evenly. Adjust seasonings and serve. Makes 8 servings as a side. Leftovers make a great lunch or snack the next day!

Note: A neat way to thinly slice fresh basil leaves: stack them, roll into logs, slice with knife, forming confetti-like shavings.

RACHAEL RAY

TOP
30

30-MINUTE MEALS

SUPER SLOPPY JOES

DEVILED
POTATO SALAD

makes 4 servings

Deviled POTATO SALAD

2 & 1/2 pounds potatoes, new or white round, peeled
  and diced

Coarse salt

1/4 medium onion

3 tablespoons prepared yellow mustard

1/2 cup mayonnaise

1 teaspoon sweet paprika

1 teaspoon hot sauce, such as Tabasco

Salt and freshly ground black pepper, to taste

2 scallions, thinly sliced, for garnish

Boil potatoes in salted water until tender, about 10 minutes. Drain and return cooked potatoes to the warm pot
to dry them out. Let potatoes stand 2 minutes, then
spread them out on a cookie sheet to quick-cool them.

In the bottom of a medium mixing bowl, grate the onion
using a hand grater. Add mustard, mayonnaise, paprika,
and hot sauce and stir to combine. Add potatoes to the
bowl and evenly distribute dressing. Season with salt and
pepper and adjust seasonings. Top with scallions.

Super **SLOPPY JOES**

1 tablespoon extra-virgin olive oil

1 & 1/4 pounds ground beef sirloin

1/4 cup brown sugar

2 to 2 & 1/2 teaspoons Montreal Steak Seasoning by McCormick

1 medium onion, chopped

1 small red bell pepper, chopped

1 tablespoon red wine vinegar

1 tablespoon Worcestershire sauce

2 cups tomato sauce

2 tablespoons tomato paste

4 crusty rolls, split, toasted, and lightly buttered

Sliced ripe tomatoes and pickles, for garnish

Heat a large skillet over medium-high heat. Add oil and beef to the pan, spreading it around to break it up. Combine brown sugar and steak seasoning, then add to skillet and combine. When meat has browned, add onion and red pepper. Reduce heat to medium and cook for 5 minutes. Add vinegar, stirring briefly to reduce, then add Worcestershire, tomato sauce and paste, stirring to combine. Reduce heat to simmer and cook 5 minutes longer.

Using a large spoon or ice cream scoop, pile meat onto toasted, buttered bun bottoms and cover with bun tops. Serve with sliced tomatoes seasoned with salt and pepper, pickles, and deviled potato salad. Have plenty of napkins on hand!

Index